'Restaurant Figures and all that Number crunching stuff'

RESTAURANT
Financial
Management

Introduction to Accounting and Finance,
for Independent Restaurants.
THE THIN RED LINE

Allen T. Mbengeranwa

Copyright © 2014 Allen Mbengeranwa

Restaurant Financial Management: introduction to accounting and finance, The Thin Red Line for independent restaurants.

ISBN: 978-1-291-85976-8

All rights reserved. This book, ebook, epub, or parts thereof, may not be reproduced in any form without permission from the publisher; exceptions are made for brief excerpts used in published reviews.

While all attempts have been made to verify the information provided in this publication, neither Author nor the Publisher assumes any responsibility for errors, omissions or contradictory interpretation of the subject matter herein. This great publication is not intended for use as a source of any form of legal, financial, emotional, personal, accounting or professional advice. This material is not a substitute or replacement of sound professional, insured advice. Please make up your own mind or engage the services of an individual or organisation willing to accept the responsibility which the author and publisher clearly will not, under any and all possible circumstances. The publisher wishes to let it be known and accepted that the information and illustrations contained herein may be subject to different geographical rules, regulations and laws. All users are advised to verify determine what local rules, regulations and laws that their independent restaurant or business may be subject to. The reader or purchaser of this work assumes responsibility for the use of the materials and information. Please accept and understand all local official and professional guides, rules, laws and regulations that govern your chosen business activity.

Contents

Contents	3
Introduction	5
Avoiding the Restaurant kiss of death	8
Optimism	11
Kitchen-Economics	13
Factors of Production *(F.O.P)*	15
Understanding Costs	18
THE STAFF MEAL	23
Productivity and Smart Automation	25
Keeping Score: Bookkeeping	28
GENERAL ACCEPTED GUIDELINES	32
A brief introduction to measurement and monitoring	35
WHY PERFORM ALL THIS MEASURING AND MONITORING?	36
CHARACTERISTICS OF MEASURING ACTIVITIES	38
Objectives of financial reporting	41
The Independent Restaurant's Stakeholders	43
Activities of the Independent Restaurant	45
SUPPLIER MARKET QUOTATION LIST	47

RECIPE DETAIL AND COST CARD	48
Application of Accounting Practices	**49**
Internal Audit	**55**
STOREROOM INVENTORY WORKSHEETS	58
Relevance of Accounting for the Chef	**59**
The Time Value of Money	**64**
Independent Restaurant Cash Flow Statement	**68**
The Independent Restaurant Balance Sheet	**73**
Independent Restaurant Income Statement	**77**
Computer and Mobile Application Programmes	**80**

Introduction

A natural instinct for survival drives us to eat, and to eat particular foods and give a wide berth to others. This is probably a basic assumption towards why we eat, prior to food hedonism. The Restaurateur learns to go beyond this bare platform and take Diners to a level of consumption that involves greater involvement of the senses. This elevation of food is said to involve taste, smell, texture, aesthetic appeal and emotional connotations, associations.

The Restaurateur may not see accounting and finance or 'the books' side of the independent restaurant as necessary to their craft or survival. The focus is usually on aspects of the job that provide great pleasure and satisfaction through creativity and expressionism by way of new dishes and ingredients. A strong dislike or feelings of disgust towards measurement and monitoring through financial and accounting systems may emanate from the misconception that such actions stifle creativity and artistic expression.

This book proposes the contrary. Reducing the number of areas that the Restaurateur has to worry about through good records and discipline frees up time and mental 'real estate' to do that which they love more and crave. It is therefore proposed that the methods and systems put forward in this book will provide some peace of mind and reassurance that feeds and nourishes creativity. Creativity which all too often stands to distinguish the great Restaurateurs from the mediocre and mundane.

The omnipresent absents of hedonism in accounting systems for the talented Restaurateur is probably a major contributor to the seemingly swift unexpected death of many an independent restaurant dream.

To improve the odds of survival, it is vital to respect, engage and practice the necessary evils of financial accounting. The Restaurateur works in a restaurant establishment which is described as being in the Hospitality industry, or more broadly, the Service Sector. The strengths of running a restaurant are numerous and unfortunately, the same factors tend to be the left heel tendon of the mighty Achilles. The reality is, very little, if anything apart from possibly a name or trademark can be protected in the food sector. Most elements of a restaurant concept can easily and legally be copied by others. These easy to duplicate items include menus, design, themes, recipes and equipment. In fact, it is a common downside that the Chef trains up an apprentice who later opens up their own establishment cooking precisely the old masters dishes, at a lower price.

There is usually no merit in taking up a licence in a sector, such as the food industry where there is little or no technology and patent protection. There are benefits to taking on a strong brand. However, the main benefits lie in the operating system which is based on good accounting systems. The downside is that the brand is usually tightly guarded, protected and monitored that the chef becomes a tiny cog in a giant machine. Lacking the genuine buzz of an independent owner-managed eatery.

Often the owner, who is technically speaking, carrying all the risk for the capital invested, does not receive a great return compared to the brand and system owner. In order to secure the capital and the great feeling of independence as well as pride of ownership, the chef will do well to implement good systems especially in the areas of finance and accounting management.

The importance of putting one's own name above the door and starting with a clean sheet means being able to control and work unrestricted on the business.

{ Introduction to Accounting and Finance,
THE THIN RED LINE
for Independent Restaurants }

Avoiding the Restaurant kiss of death

Keeping records and measuring the financial health of the restaurant, using cold hard numbers, will help protect the restaurant from the stealth problems faced by many independent restaurateurs. This is probably the equivalent of carbon monoxide poisoning in terms of the likely fatal result of a lack of safeguards and regular monitoring. Blissful ignorance is no longer an acceptable form of defence when the time comes to conduct an inquest into the restaurant.

The excessive drawing of capital by the owner, unchecked, usually leads to the restaurants early demise. A restaurant is a cash rich business and handling or touching all that money is very tempting. Any business drained of vital Working Capital will not survive. It has been observed by many professionals especially bank managers and venture capitalists or professional investors, that this 'death by draining' has two causes. Firstly, a lack of understanding about finance by the owner and managers, and then secondly, no self-discipline about money.

The information and illustrations in the book help to highlight the effects of drawing working capital and assist the restaurateur who may find it difficult to engage in some delayed gratification when it comes to the rewards for starting up the restaurant business.

Owning a restaurant has been known to bestow upon the owner a glamorous social status. Restaurants are associated with romance and the ability to create an uncanny buzz and provide a facility for people to experience euphoric spasms. This can make it difficult to remain disciplined and overcome normal objectivity while avoiding falling victim to many errors that blight beginners.

Some chefs or restaurateurs view themselves as adventurous rule breakers who will not be hemmed in by standard practices. However, all who have succeeded will know that when it comes to financial and accounting management, following the rules is the only option. There is no way round understanding successful traditional methods.

At times some actions in managing a restaurant can be done with good intentions. However, only with hindsight and third-party explanation can the mystery be unravelled. This misallocation of capital when times are good and money is awash leads to waste and eventual reckoning as seemingly, what goes around, does not always come around before it's too late.

There is a theory put forward by is namesake labelled, Schumpeters' 'creative destruction'. The interpretation suggests that inefficient restaurants disappear and more productive restaurateurs survive. It does not seem to be creative talent that ensures survival but effective measuring and monitoring.

Poor knowledge of what's financially going on in the restaurant may lead to the chef loading up with too much debt when times are good and in the same way as leveraged buyouts struggle in downturns, the restaurant struggles.

Another common practice by the less than financially knowledgeable restaurateur is to implement a seemingly good survival plan. This plan involves looking at the empty restaurant tables and deciding that the solution is to maintain sales by discounting current prices and sacrificing margins to preserve volumes. When most tables are empty, the chef still has to ensure that the oven and lights are kept on and paid for.

The chef also needs to keep a good eye on promises made to the banks. This is easier and more accurate to do with financial tools. The effect of raising prices when consumers knowingly have less money to spend is also noticeable.

Normally there are rash decisions made by the restaurateur without measurement and monitoring of finances in place. These often include cutbacks on staff, engaging in a refurbishment programme and other capital expenditures in and around the restaurant.

Restaurant operators with experience know that measuring and monitoring financial activity will eventually show those who are lucky and will eventually fail when economic times get tough and differentiate those chefs who know what they are doing and will survive. The strong practitioners will get stronger and the weak will only serve to supply the successful with anecdotes.

Optimism

The Restaurateur must remain optimistic. Optimism in a world where the failure rate is dangerously high and the prospect of success is very slim indeed. However, without optimism and faith there would be no pioneers that have blazed a wriggly path to restaurant utopia. An ideal place where even after the founding fathers have long gone, the restaurant remains alive and kicking.

The journey to start a restaurant begins from the Restaurateurs' self-belief and optimism. Born of confidence and propelled ambition, this optimism is a prelude to the creation of many unique new jobs and kitchen inventions. To sustain this optimism, it is sometimes necessary to base it on a sound foundation. Many restaurants have not been brilliant or avant-garde but relatively well managed and monitored using sound financial accounting techniques. It is up to the chef to decide what the future holds and how they intend to address the upcoming events. This book offers a basis to progress with optimism and hope instead of looking at the future with eyes filled with fear.

Adrenaline rushes sometimes experienced by restaurateurs can lead to reckless behaviour. Irrational actions will result in a disaster. A calculated leap of faith through the good use of financial measurement and monitoring techniques. Devoid of sensible hedging prior to action, the chef acts as though they lack sufficient knowledge in the fast paced game of modern capitalism and will unfortunately loose.

To build and maintain a solid business, as the clichés go, it is necessary to start from the ground up, from the feet up, start from the bottom, build a solid foundation and so on. Getting the basics right is usually the first step to survival. Efficiency can be achieved and time saved by simply elevating service to service or day to day tasks into the independent restaurants financial activities.   In order to determine what is available to offer customers, for example, the Chef does a quick stock-take and comes up with a specials menu. In the same spirit, looking at the supplier market quotation list determines what is currently offering the returns or consistency. This behaviour can filter through to the methods of calculating costs and their subsequent impact on the Income Statement and Balance Sheet position.

Using a recipe detail and cost template will also get down to the nuts and bolts of ingredients and allow the Chef or Restaurateur to assess the impact of market fluctuations on price to the yield and contribution margins. Sufficient emphasis is placed on internal financial accounting, management accounting of the independent restaurant for the chef to keep his or her head above the water with the calmness and poise of a plump mallard duck.

There is no specific order in which to go through this book, however, the recommendation is that the readers assesses for themselves and start where they are comfortable. This may be in an area of greater knowledge or on a subject where more inspiration is needed. This is not a prescriptive initiative, rather a basic guide with a significant level of detail to enable positive decision making and offer some sort of reassurance that there are no barriers to Independent Restaurant financial discovery.

Kitchen-Economics

Kitchen-Economics refers to acquired knowledge of kitchen economic principles and policies, as used by chefs within a food production facility with sales direct to the consumer such as a restaurant or caterer.

Kitchen economics is essentially the same as business standard economics with factors of production. At the moment, it is acceptable that the ordinary Restaurateur does not need to understand the 'formal' financial matters. Traditionally, the Chef has concentrated on the kitchen or back of house side of the restaurant and formed a partnership with others to provide the front of house and overall management.

Many chefs pride themselves in being artists and need to 'concentrate' on creating new dishes and the people management of kitchen staff. However, modern cookery schools now include in their curriculum the 'numbers side' of running a kitchen. A busy dining room does not necessarily translate into profitable restaurant.

In order to understand and progress with cooking, technology and good practice both need to be applied beyond trend setting with molecular gastronomy. Traditionally, it was enough to divide the cost of an ingredient by the number of portions and multiply by four to get a bench mark of some sort. Today, and in the future, more detailed bench marks and analysis tools are needed from the bottom up.

The Thin Red Line of Small Business Financial Management aims to provide a starting point for the Restaurateur with the application of good business principles for benchmarking and self-management. Kitchen-economics tackles the issues of performance measurement for analysis and direction based on actual activities. The Restaurateur who wants to improve will start by measuring how they are doing now in order to set a direction for the future.

> *Marco Pierre White famously charged £25 for a portion chips, as a side order for one!*

Factors of Production *(F.O.P)*

Within the professional kitchen environment, F.O.P is an economic term rarely used and it describes the inputs that are used in the production of customer goods and front of house services in an attempt to make an economic profit for the proprietor or investors. As in other industries, F.O.P includes land, labour, capital and entrepreneurship.

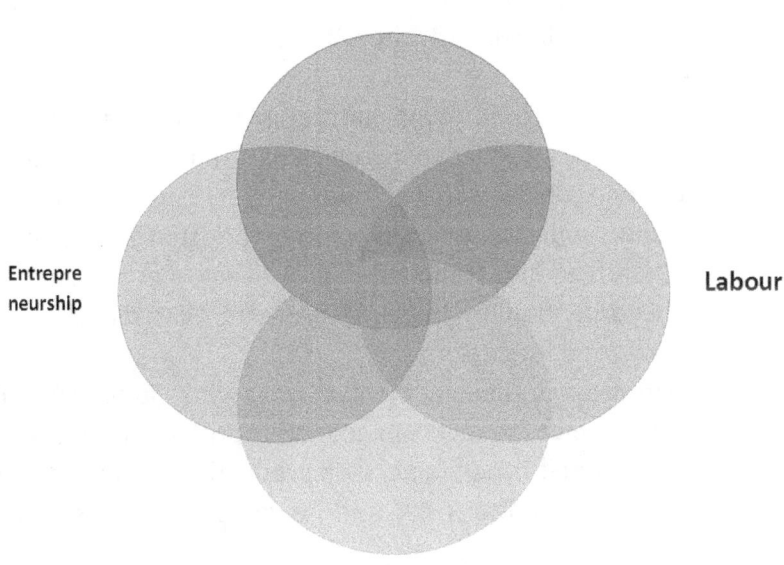

F.O.P is known to encompass all the inputs needed to produce a customer's goods namely food and/or service. Economics is not unique to the professional kitchen, as a study, academic principles have rarely been significantly applied to the kitchen. Although man has needed to consume in order to survive over time, the kitchen is not really considered a centre for economic analysis. The experience gained by many domestic goddesses over time, and passed down to the next generation has formed the bedrock of kitchen policies and philosophies. Comparatively, the kitchen tends to produce less in terms of scale relative to other industries or professions.

Nonetheless, the Restaurateur needs to understand the formality and labels attached to the historic informalities of kitchens.

Land refers to all things natural in resources and ingredients such as fish, vegetables, or woodchips used in the production of an economic good or plate of food.

Labour, typically includes all the work that the kitchen staff, waiting staff, administration staff and all levels of the organisation, with the exception of the entrepreneur, that directly relate to producing food for customers.

Entrepreneur, usually the chef or the individual who takes an idea and attempts to make an economic profit from the restaurant by combining all other factors of production. The entrepreneur also assumes all the risks and rewards of the restaurant or business.

Capital is all the foods and machinery used to produce a good or service and relates to all that is needed for the customer experience at the restaurant and any other means by which they connect.

The F.O.P are usually blended in various amounts with the entrepreneurship element being the binding factor. The plethora of restaurant types illustrates that F.O.P required in varying amounts and combination. In addition, it is important to understand that F.O.P are inputs to the production process and the finished goods or services are the outputs, in essence.

The above description of F.O.P as inputs and the subsequent outputs, distils the business or restaurant operations model. The menu of a Glasgow Chip shop as illustrated on page 24, perhaps forms the best and simplest example of F.O.P in play. The Chip shop prices are basically the output, with the inputs forming a direct base for the later. The link is clear and obvious between the fish and the potatoes with the Battered fillets and chips. Comparing these chip shop staples over time, perhaps gives a better understanding of modern Kitchen-economics.

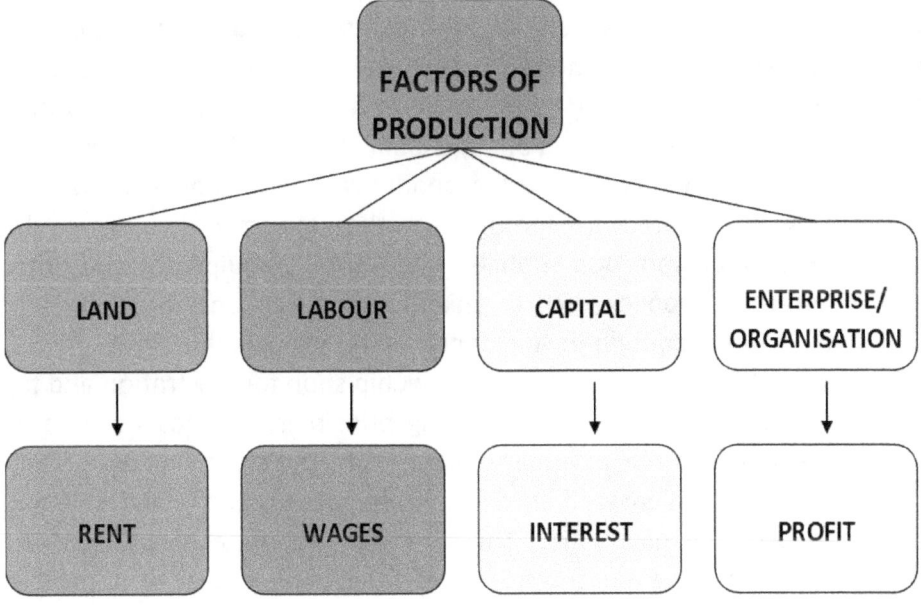

[*Parkinson's Law*
'Work expands to fill the time
available for its completion']

Understanding Costs

If the chef is to be considered a professional craftsman, he or she must understand costs. Business 'gurus' insist that one cannot be successful in maintaining a living without a complete grasp of all things relating to their chosen enterprise or endeavour. A critical element of this is understanding Costs. The Chip Shop owner in Glasgow has to understand how much s/he can charge for a bag of chips and how much they can expect to pay for a bag of potatoes.

Business models vary, however, for the professional chef, costs can also be defined by industry standards as a value of money, cash or otherwise, that has been used to produce a customer's food and is no longer available for use for anything else. The Glasgow Chip Shop, usually denotes the accounting cost as the monetary value of expenditures. The food and concept may be different throughout the industry however, the expenditure on food supplies, staff labour, equipment and other non-food supplies such as cleaning materials and disposables in the form of containers and condiments, remains the same.

Still referring to the Glasgow Chip shop for illustration and tax purposes plus general accounting principles. The costs are easily identified as the monetary value that appears on invoices from suppliers and entered onto employee payslips and Inland Revenue reports plus payments. This all relates to the chef and not just solely creating amazing plates of food. The challenge is then to create experiences for the customer with the minimum monetary value in proportion to the revenue received from customers.

The traditional, classically trained chef does not look kindly on insolence when it comes to food and time wasting as this is a representation of some of the accounting costs not being transferred to the customer or benefiting staff and wasted. All kitchen staff, from the Commis at every section, via the Chef de Partie to the Sous Chef are expected to learn and understand that there is a zero waste policy. This is often an unwritten rule but central to many doctrines of cooking and kitchen management.

Grace and favour from the Chef or owners comes from inadvertently keeping accounting costs down in order to:

a. Maximise profit

b. Foster creativity and team work as someone may use your 'waste' for another dish or the staff meal.

The great Chef Auguste Escoffier and his partner Caesar Ritz are reported to have been sacked from the Savoy hotel for 'taking kickbacks' from suppliers running into the millions of pounds at the expense of their employer. Using the kitchens' influence for personal financial gain is fraudulent and frowned upon.

That aside, more recently, another great Chef Pierre Koffman or was it Fergus Henderson is known to have coined the phrase, "From the pig, eat everything but the oink!" As a business philosophy, this usually translates into profit, especially when a major cost factor, ingredients, is often variable by weight. Trimming and 'feeding the bin' is a clear practice of binning the chef's or owner's money away.

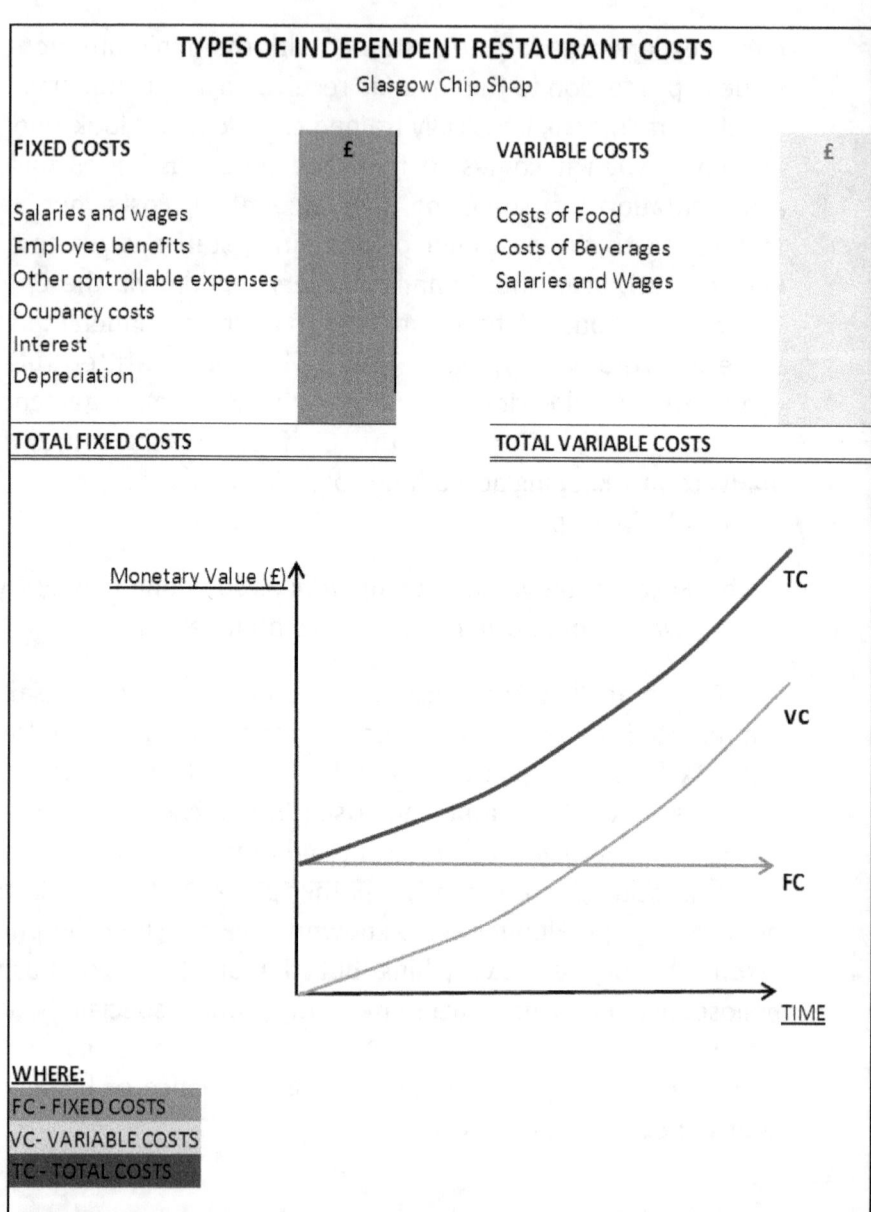

GLASGOW CHIP SHOP
CALCULATING COSTS

CALCULATING FOOD COST PERCENTAGE

Food Cost % = $\dfrac{\text{Food Cost[FC]}}{\text{Food Sales[FS]}}$

Food Cost % = $\dfrac{\text{£[FC]}}{\text{£[FS]}}$

Food Cost % =

CALCULATING LABOUR COST

Salaries and Wages	£
Employee Benefits	£
Labour Cost	£

CALCULATING BEVERAGE COST PERCENTAGE

Beverage Cost % = $\dfrac{\text{Beverage Cost [BC]}}{\text{Beverage Sales [BS]}}$

Beverage Cost % = $\dfrac{\text{£[BC]}}{\text{£[BS]}}$

Beverage Cost % =

CALCULATING LABOUR COST PERCENTAGE

Labour Cost % = $\dfrac{\text{Labour Cost [LC]}}{\text{Total Sales [TC]}}$

Labour Cost % = $\dfrac{\text{£[LC]}}{\text{£[TC]}}$

Labour Cost % =

GLASGOW CHIP SHOP
CALCULATING COSTS

CALCULATING OVERHEAD COSTS

Overhead Costs	£
Other Controllable Expenses	£
Occupancy Costs	£
Interest	£
Depreciation	£
TOTAL OVERHEAD COSTS	**£**

CALCULATING OVERHEAD COST PERCENTAGE

$$\text{Overhead Cost Percentage \%} = \frac{\text{Total Overhead Costs}}{\text{Total Sales}}$$

OC% = _____

CALCULATING PRIME COST

Total Cost of Sales	£
Labour Cost	£
PRIME COST	**£**

CALCULATING PRIME COST PERCENTAGE

$$\text{Prime Cost \%} = \frac{\text{Prime Cost [PC]}}{\text{Total Sales [TS]}}$$

$$\text{Prime Cost \%} = \frac{£[PC]}{£[TS]}$$

Prime Cost % = _____

NOTES:-

CALCULATING PROFIT PERCENTAGE

$$\text{Profit Percent} = \frac{\text{Restaurant Profit [RP]}}{\text{Total Sales [TS]}}$$

$$\text{Profit \%} = \frac{£[RP]}{£[TS]}$$

PROFIT % = _____

CALCULATING TOTAL COST PERCENT

Prime Cost %	=	PC%
Overhead Cost %	=	OC%
Profit %	=	P%
TOTAL COST %	**=**	

VARIABLE RATE [VR]

$$VR = \frac{\text{Variable Cost [VC]}}{\text{Sales [S]}}$$

VR = _____

CONTRIBUTION RATE [CR]

CR = 1 - [VR]

CR = _____

BREAK EVEN [BE]

$$BE = \frac{\text{Fixed Cost [FC]}}{\text{Contribution rate [CR]}}$$

$$BE = \frac{[FC]}{[CR]}$$

BE = _____

The Staff Meal

Often the Chef is expected to 'look after' the staff by providing lunch and dinner free of charge. It is considered an additional bonus for staff to be fed at work as they 'top-up' their wages from the savings made from not spending their own money purchasing food during the working week.

As customers traditionally expect the best on their plate, all the trimmings are expected to go towards the staff meal. In essence, the customer is subsidising the staff meal as the price per plate is calculated based on the supplier weight, pre-presentation trim.

In a nutshell, awareness of price and price changes, as illustrated in this instance on page 24 by the Chip-shop prices in Glasgow, drives home the importance of a 'waste-free' culture within the professional kitchen. Knowledge of costs and profit elevates the traditional cook into a professional chef. Cooking for passion is admirable, cooking for profit is professional.

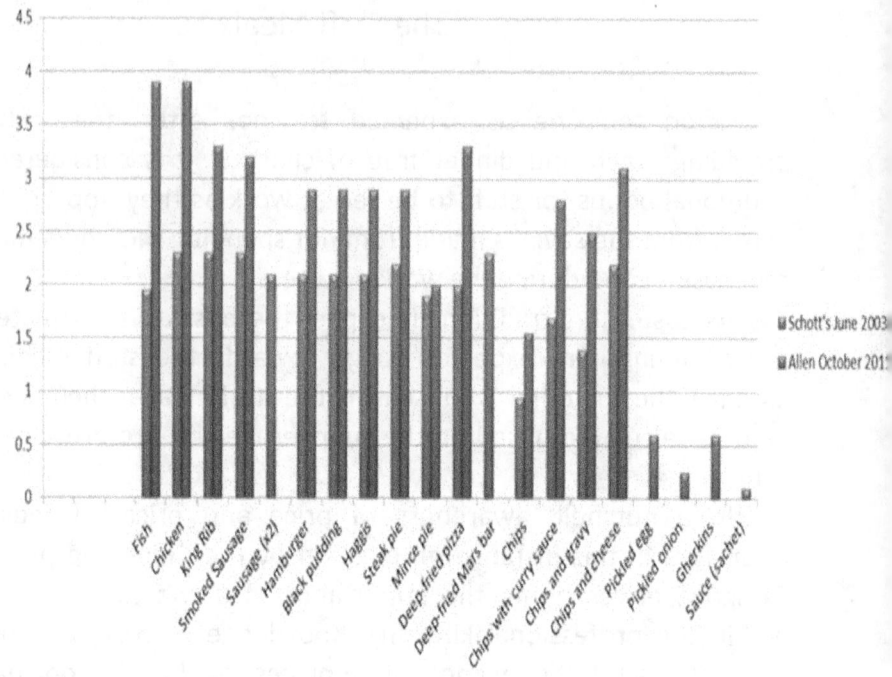

Chip shop prices in Glasgow

The Mis-Education of the Professional Chef - Allen Mbengeranwa

> 'Seek the first principles, when you lack money, what you must do is think' – Ernest Rutherford (1871-1937). He split the Atom.

Productivity and Smart Automation

Kitchens are supposed to run like machines with people there only to serve the process, to carry out the necessary steps of fabrication where produce enters the system at one end and is turned into plates of food at the other end for paying guests.

The ideal situation is that the Chef does not engage in mindless automations working to service the machinery of food production. To be sufficiently useful, the Chef needs to show what can be referred to as Smart automation. The difference between the former and the later forms of automation relies on two aspects. The first is that the Chef is adaptable and the second being that the Chef is willing and able to acquire new skills.

The above rests on the premise that stuff learned tomorrow is based on stuff learned today. This engages the brain at the pivotal moment where the mindless automaton Chef becomes the smart and productive automaton Chef. The robotic reference provides parity to consistency and homage to reliability in the eyes of customers. The preferred state of automaton Chef, smart, relies on the utilisation of skills and reflexes acquired over the years.

Furthermore, the smart automaton Chef learns from others 'how we do things in this kitchen' and adapts. This is probably made easier if the chef has a certain degree of confidence in their desire to become a better automaton.

What does it mean to be smart, adaptable and being prepared to learn new skills in a professional environment?

The kitchen environment, rather, the professional kitchen environment provides a unique opportunity to prove ones' adaptability or willingness to learn new skills. Most chefs who have had to learn on the job will tell anyone willing to listen a story or two about what it means to learn quickly.

The professional kitchen environment creates a special environment in which the young new chef may not have encountered before. Being hired usually means taking up someone else's position where that person may have left or been promoted to a new position where they themselves have to learn new skills quickly and deliver results, fast. This scenario unfortunately means that there is often no one to hold the new chefs hand and incubate them during the crucial and fragile learning phase.

The phase when the chef has to listen and ask busy colleagues the seemingly stupid questions they may have. The phase when the chef has to listen and pay attention to the equipment, the check calls from the Abouyeur or Announcer; requests for timings from 'team mates'; listen for orders to move out of the way; listen to their own heart beat or legs and instincts to monitor how the body is coping. Listen to the little voice in their suddenly small head that is searching through the chef's mind palace in order to find a similarly inspired historical experience in which to take comfort and refuge from the external chaos and provide some sort of unspecified compass.

In the meantime, the chef has yet to learn to distinguish, for example, the smell of burning bread from all the other new smells that are bombarding the now flared nasal cavity and all the sensors that are engaged in smelling. So, sheepishly progress must be made, assuming a continuation of the elementary toast task, by this time the chef has to redo the toast as the first attempt resulted in sacrilege, now feeling suddenly inadequate and ashamed at failing such a penal task while wondering how many people are passing judgement. As first impressions go, this is certainly not the worst, which makes failure all the more telling. Moving swiftly on.

The idea that egotistical and pompous behavioural characteristics as well as delusions of grandeur may hinder the chef being adaptable and learning new methods from 'less able' new colleagues comes only from experience. It emanates again from the assumption that tasks learned tomorrow are based on tasks learned today. It is also only logical to say that, in a less philosophical way, tasks learned today are based on tasks learned yesterday.

How we learn and adapt is all very personal. Smart professional chefs will learn to reflect upon their work and review any effort, like most professionals. This practice is easily done through the keeping and reviewing of good records based on detailed measurement and monitoring techniques, preferably based on accurate numbers and methods detailed in this book.

Simply put, being productive or working smart is simply a measure or comparison against seemingly historic stupidity and obvious wastefulness plus blatant disregard for the common sense approach in addition to a lack of sound judgement or training.

Keeping Score: Bookkeeping.

Bookkeeping is one of the building blocks of accounting and involves the bread and butter mechanics used to record and gather the Independent Restaurant's business and financial transactions. To relate and contextualise some of the terms or descriptions of actions, often it is necessary to delve into the past to look at the origins of some of the practices. Not much has changed in some respects. As an example, we all still need to eat and businesses have been making a profit, sole trader or otherwise since time immemorial.

Imagine a young professional, Mr Cust Omer, enters the Glasgow Chip Shop and orders a portion of large breaded haddock and hand cut triple fried chips with garden mushy peas for two at £12.50. the Independent restaurant will view this bread and butter encounter as something similar to what follows below.

- Mr Cust Omer asks the Chef for a large haddock and chips with mushy peas for two and promises to pay £12.50.

- Chef believes Mr Cust Omer will pay and deep fries fish and chips plus prepares the mushy peas.

- Chef is right handed and passes fish and chips plus mushy peas to Mr Cust Omer's right hand side across the fry counter.

- The value or benefit is passed from the Chefs Right hand side to the corresponding right hand side of Mr Cust Omer across the fry counter.

- The Independent Restaurant then proceeds to record the actions manually in a system, a form of keeping score otherwise known as bookkeeping.

- For the suppliers to the restaurant, the opposite is true.

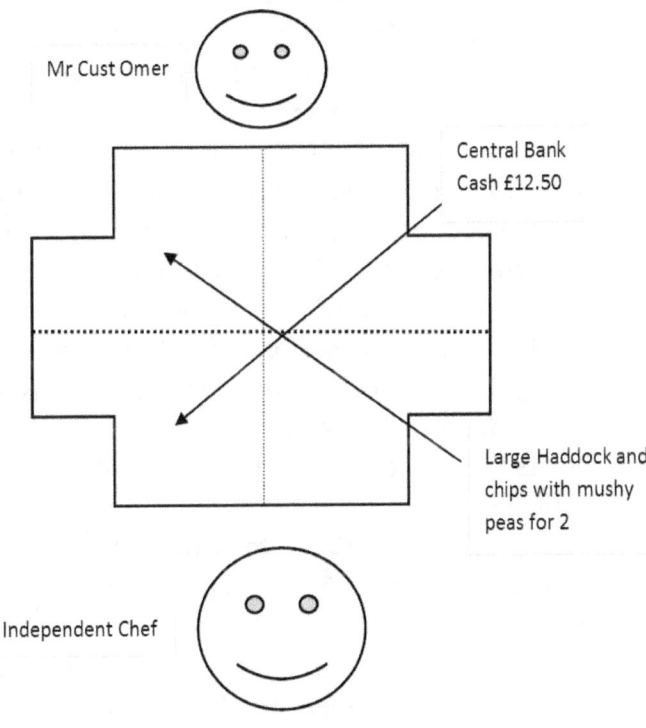

The word Ledger comes from the word Ledge, unsurprisingly, as in window ledge where the business book used to be kept. This has a "T" layout or format on each page which is assigned to an individual account. This page is split equally down the middle to form two folios or pages, much the same as A4 becomes A5. At the top of each page is a bold line where the titles are written to identify the actions.

For the Chef, one side of the page in the ledger is entitled Mr Cust Omer above the "T" forming a horizontal line at the top and the other side is labelled Glasgow Chip Shop.

On the Left hand side of Mr Cust Omer's account, also known formally as the Debit side as bookkeeping evolved from Latin. The word Debit comes from the Latin *Debeo* which means 'I am owed'. This can also be described as 'the benefit goes to' in modern language. This side is where the entry is made by the Restaurateur. In addition to this entry or recording, the rest of the information denotes the date, the name of the independent restaurant 'Glasgow Chip Shop' and the amount under a column headed 'pounds' or with the symbol '£'.

In the same ledger or book, there is another account headed 'Glasgow Chip Shop' on the next page. This is also in the form of a "T" as described above. On this page, in the right hand column headed Credit, the Restaurateur records the corresponding entry. Suffice to say credit also comes from Latin. This time the word is *Credeo* which translates to 'I believe'. Once again, the date is entered, the name of the source, Mr Cust Omer and the same amount paid.

This is how the single book or ledger records the agreement between the customer and the restaurant when food is ordered. The Independent restaurant is lending or offering in exchange for value food and beverages to the customer. The Chef or Restaurateur is willing to engage, trust and believe that at the end of the meal, Mr Cust Omer will pay for the dining experience.

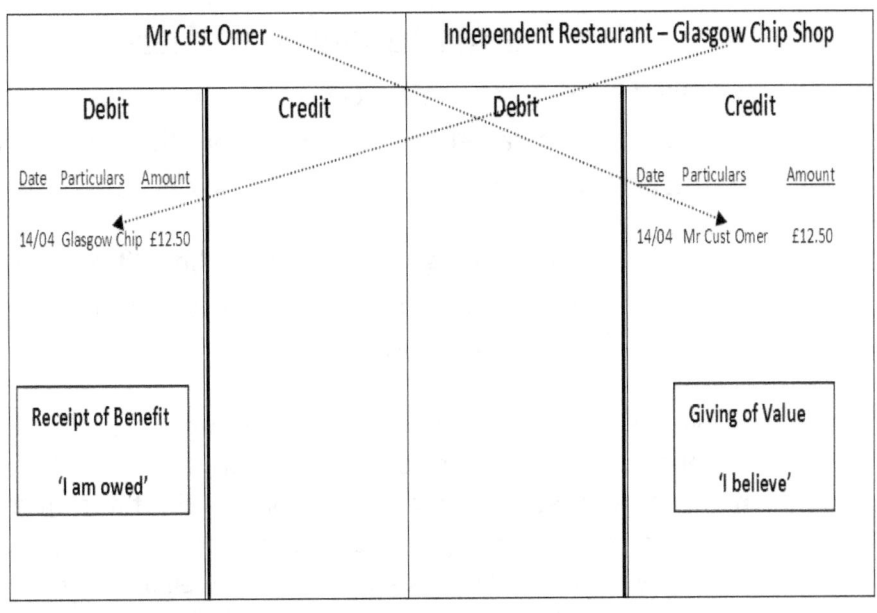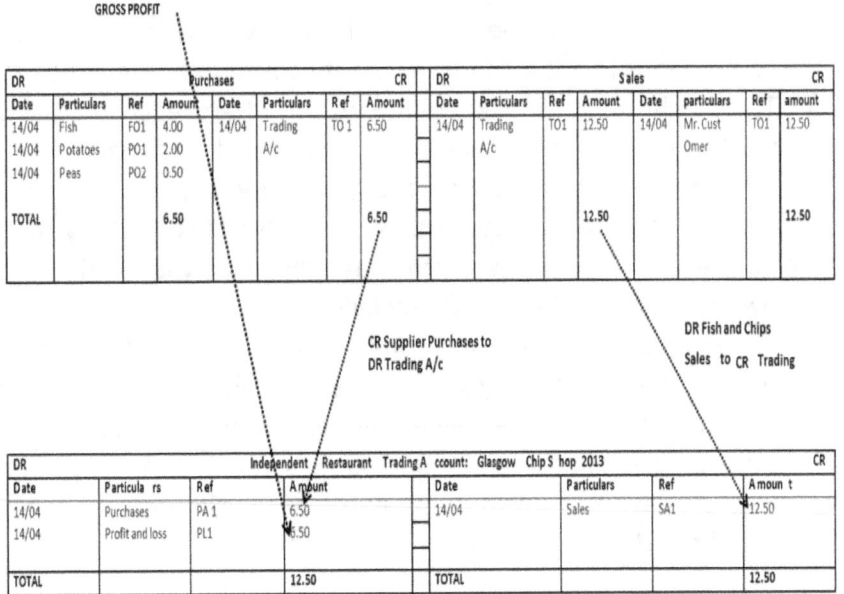

Restaurant Financial Management 31

General Accepted Guidelines

- Debit Entry to the left receives the benefit or value and records the asset or expense for the Independent restaurant.

- Credit Entry to the right passes on the benefit or value and so records the action as a liability or item of revenue for the Independent restaurant.

If we are to be pedantic about keeping the score in business, that is bookkeeping, we can relate to an unrelated law of physics from the most respected Albert Einstein which states that "for every action, there's an equal and opposite reaction". However, seeing as we are name-dropping we might as well do it properly.

The idea of using a double entry bookkeeping system as opposed to the single entry system is widely reported to have come about in 1494 thanks to an Italian monk called Luca Pacioli. The single entry bookkeeping system where each transaction is written down once is useful even though it has drawbacks. This system lacks the ability to easily identify any mistakes or show lending and borrowings. This system also fails to show the value of previous purchases in the last financial year which are still owned or in use the next financial year.

At the heart of the monk's system is the fact that every transaction, whatever form it takes, involves the giving of value and the receiving of said value. A perfect system observed in 1494 for the basis of accounting and sounds very much like the one Mr Einstein gave the world in the name of physics or science to great acclaim. Hence in order to get a more accurate picture, Pacioli advocated the recording of every transaction twice. As a Double entry into the book from the window ledge.

The independent Restaurateur engages in business and all concerned assume that this will continue for the foreseeable future. We all assume that like any other business, the Glasgow Chip shop will continue trading in fish and chips plus accompaniments. The tried and tested business model operates along the lines of the Chef making purchases of ingredients and other items from various suppliers, prepares and cooks to perfection any orders from Mr Cust Omer and friends for cash sales.

As the Independent restaurant business is likely to have more than one customer and supplier, it is more efficient to use Nominal Accounts. This is an account that only represents value and not an actual physical asset which is central to the less effective single entry bookkeeping system. The Nominal account only exists in name only, that is, Nominal.

The Sales of the restaurant are always Credits as they GIVE VALUE to the business. Consequently, the Purchases are always Debits as they RECEIVE VALUE from suppliers. The objective of the restaurant is to make a profit which is essentially the result of measuring the difference between the sales and the purchases; hopefully the former is greater than the latter. Should the opposite occur, then the independent business has made an unfortunate loss.

The above is a basic Gross Profit for the restaurant. Using three nominal accounts, two of which are Purchases and Sales, by introducing a third, Trading Account, a more professional image appears. The purchases are debited in the Purchase account with the Sales credited as cash in the sales account. The Trading account then brings it all together. The objective of the restaurant is to make a profit and not a loss. The outcome is then recorded in the Profit and Loss account. At this point, the Independent restaurant keeps a score of profit as Gross profit which the Restaurateur, as described above, arrives at by collating all the sales for the period and subtracting the cost of said sales. This is all easily illustrated in the Trading account. Clearly, in accordance with the Monks' principles, any amount needed to "balance" this Trading account may be considered a surplus to activities and therefore gross profit.

The Independent Restaurant, in this case the Glasgow Chip Shop acquires expenses also known as overheads when the Chef or Restaurateur operates the business. These expenses may have their own individual accounts in the bookkeeping ledger. These include items such as the rent account, tax account, wages account and advertising account. Luckily for the person responsible for bookkeeping and the owners, the expenses use the same rules or guidelines as the Purchases and Sales accounts in double entry bookkeeping principles. Once again, the account giving value is credited and any account receiving value is debited.

Manually, in the 'T' account, assets and expenses are recorded as debit entries on the left hand side as this is owned by the restaurant and needed to settle the restaurants liabilities for example, cash in the till. Credit corresponds on the right hand side of the 'T' account to record the liabilities and much needed revenue.

> *As to methods there may be a million and then some, but principles are few. The man who grasps the principles can successfully select his own methods. The man, who tries methods, ignoring principles, is sure to have trouble –* **Ralph Waldo Emerson**

A brief introduction to measurement and monitoring.

1. The Chef or restaurateur should endeavour to avoid being lazy. Financial management should be as simple as possible, but not any simpler. Sometimes the requirements may seem complex and unnecessary, the chef or owner cannot avoid the complexity, and they have to deal with it.

2. The focus should be on the whole financial process. It is easy for the chef or manager to focus on their area or part of the business in a way that creates significant problems and issues later. Effective and accurate measures are based on the whole process and not just part of it. This is much the same way as the Beatles achieved greater fame and fortune as a whole. As separate entities and not as a team, Paul, John, George and Ringo fell far short of their collective greatness. This should stand as an example to avoid sub-optimisation of the restaurant.

3. Instead of an internal approach, the Chef or proprietor should measure something that matters to the customer. This is easier achieved when the objective is to get things right the first time and is usually a very cost effective modus operandi which provides great substance for

management mantra which is readily adopted by general staff.

4. The chef and restaurateur should assume, with good reason, that customers, staff and suppliers are only human and will try and game the system. This may be a contentious idea but it is Hypothesis driven. This provides an opportunity for the chef be proved wrong, nobody loses and everyone's a winner.

Why perform all this measuring and monitoring?

- To provide information to enable the chef to make economic decisions.

- To evaluate business decisions affecting the continued operations of the independent restaurant.

- Provides useful information to form the basis of discussions on compensation and pay as well as promotion and rankings.

- This information is needed by the investors and banks to assess the viability of the restaurant.

- Makes available information for taxation and duty reports including investigations.

- May also be requested by suppliers when considering extending lines of credit.

Additional universal benefits of all the Independent Restaurant Financial measuring and monitoring

1. Ensures consistency and monitoring for any red and green flags to independent operations.

2. Regularity. Using regular accounting periods provides a rhythm that gives security.

3. Using low levels of basic details ensures the reports and activities are manageable and not over whelming.

4. A high level of accuracy is easily achieved from simple tasks. The result is reliable information.

5. The chef or owner may save money by identification and quick review of good information.

6. In addition to the above, the restaurants money can also be saved by performing some of the tasks in-house before engaging the services of an accounting firm.

Generally, good measurement is useful when tailored to a particular business and in this case, the independent restaurant sectors' particular issues at that point in time. The use of recipe detail and cost cards as well as store room inventory sheets in industry specific and highly relevant.

For the users, useful information has to be accurate and based of detailed analysis which is easy to achieve in a restaurant and also have an analysis or some form of commentary as to what the numbers say.

In the fast paced independent restaurant sector, good measurement makes a world of difference for the chef and owners as well as banks and investors in their efforts to understand the true causes of results and highlighting the road to possible improvement. If encountering problems before, changing measurement and monitoring techniques can be the difference between swimming and sinking.

Characteristics of measuring activities

Using financial information and numbers alone may cloud the objectives of financial measuring and monitoring activities of the independent restaurant. Most Chef Patrons and Restaurateurs enter the world of professional cookery for reasons other than money. It stands to reason that in order for the measures to be followed through with heart and determination, they, the measures, should not be solely related to revenue. An example of insular measurement would be if the Chef or Manager uses Gross profit as a percentage of sales.

This does not fully communicate the nature of the independent restaurant. Instead of the above, a more tangible measure is something that is not related to money alone. This can be along the lines of profit per hour based on staff work hours or profit per customer. Using a non-revenue item as a point of reference tends to provide more usefulness from all the work.

This is important if the Chef believes they are in the business of satisfying paying customers.

A man by the name of Vilfredo Pareto may not obviously be of apparent importance to the restaurateur. However, before Mr. Pareto died on the nineteenth of August 1923, he had observed that only 20% of his pea pods in his garden managed to produce a staggering 80% of all his peas! Furthermore, the Pareto principle was named after the great man himself. Among the popular applications of the principle, the Restaurateur and Professional Chef might find it interesting that it has been observed that a power law or Pareto Distribution exists. This claims that, for example, 80% of an independent restaurants profits emanate from 20% of its customers. There is also a further claim that 80% of the restaurants customer complaints come from 20% of its customers.

Measuring and monitoring financial and accounting activity can help identify such conclusions as above and many Restaurateurs will have an easier task of producing significant results in terms of profitability by focusing on the most effective areas, not that the rest should be ignored. This ability of measures, if used diligently, to highlight the less obvious will make it easier for Chefs' to survive tough trading environments.

The second notable characteristic of useful measures is that they are incredibly specific and accurate in relation to the particular independent restaurant and based on its concept, its individual customer demographic. Generalising on this subject does not provide accurate results which are useful. Using published data from industry wide studies may include a diverse range of establishments such as franchises and fast food outlets with multiple sites, who also consider themselves as restaurants.

There is also a danger of comparing the relatively new independent restaurant to long established entities that have acquired their freeholds and generate income from other revenue streams such s book sales, consultation and overnight money market activities. A characteristic of some successful Avant Garde independent restaurant is that they are able to attract cheap and free labour which the relatively new entrant may not.

Objectives of financial reporting

It is easy for the Chef and Restaurateur to understand and appreciate financial statements and financial reporting plus accounting practices once it is accepted that there are certain concepts fundamental to accounting. All the work done within the independent restaurant should be prepared to agreed guidelines. These guidelines are based upon the wider generally accepted objectives of financial reporting that also apply to the chef or proprietor and restaurateur.

The owners may never feel the need or inclination to share their financial activity with anyone, however, in these our economic times, the odds are it may be a necessity for one reason or another to cooperate and work as part of a team with others. No one starts or takes over an independent restaurant because they want to prepare financial statements, however, just as a health and safety system is vital to successful operations, and so is an accounting system.

Anyway, the objectives as outlined by the International Accounting Standards Board or similar is that business financial reporting, even for the small independent restaurant, is to make available material information that is useful for making business and economic decisions.

These decisions are made by existing investors, such as the Chef and potential investors and creditors, usually the local bank plus other users who make rational investment, open credit facilities to the restaurant and similar decisions.

Another important factor is the assessment of cash inflows and outflows to the independent restaurant by, once again, existing and potential money investors mainly, as well as the sometimes needed creditors among others.

Finally, there is the need to identify the independent restaurants economic resources, the claims to those resources including leases and the effect that transactions, events such as party functions or repossessions and circumstances unforeseen and possibly more like known but unexpected to the Restaurateurs, have on these economic resources.

The Independent Restaurant's Stakeholders

A stakeholder is described as an individual, such as the Chef, or group that has legitimate interest in a company. Even for the small business, a corporate stakeholder is said to be a person or group that can affect or indeed be affected by the actions of a business.

Furthermore, internal stakeholders are groups within the independent restaurant or people who work directly within the business especially members of staff such as the kitchen porter or bar person, owners, possibly the Chef and investors.

In addition to the above, extended stakeholders are outside people or groups who are mutually exclusive to employees and are not directly working within the independent restaurant business, as in some situations, but are somehow affected by the decisions of the restaurant and they include, but not limited to suppliers, trade unions, customers, creditors and government departments.

Activities of the Independent Restaurant

It seems odd to formally describe what a restaurant does. The views may be different but it is essential to enhance the understanding of what is actually happening within the independent restaurant.

The day to day activities of the restaurant can be divided into operating and non-operating activities. The former includes the preparation and production of meals and sales of beverages as well as the service or delivery to customers of the Chef's efforts in addition to the collection of payment for services rendered to the customers. Curiously, this may also involve interest on loans with other entities such as money in the bank or ninety-day money market payments.

The latter, although also important, seems not to involve the day to day bread and butter tasks but rather more to do with independent restaurant owner or manger decisions and activities such as investments and finance.

For an independent restaurant on a small to medium scale, investment activities include purchases or sales of assets including equipment in the form of new stoves or commercial blenders, land or buildings or as mentioned, money market type assets. it is highly unlikely however, loans made or paid to suppliers and customers also constitute this element of investment activity. It is not beyond the independent restaurateur to get involved in mergers and acquisitions by choice or otherwise. Once again, this is also an investment activity.

The second and final element of non-operating activities relates to financing activities. It is normal for the independent operator to require external help with the venture from investors or banks in the form of cash inflows. In the same light outflows of cash as dividends to any shareholders are also financial non-operating activities. Most of this activity appears to happen on the balance sheet of the restaurant and incorporates the nature of equity and long term liabilities of the entity.

Supplier Market Quotation List

EN PLACE	ITEM	PAR	TO ORDER	SUPPLIER QUOTES				
				A	B	C	D	E
	POTATOES							
	Chipper							
	Wedges							
	FISH							
	Cod							
	Plaice							
	Haddock							
	Monkfish							
	POULTRY							
	1/4 LEGS							
	Brest							
	Pie							
	SHELFISH							
	Lobster							
	Crab							
	Musles							
	Scallops							
	Prawns							
	Meat							
	Pork Sausage							
	Pork Pie							
	1/4 Burger							
	CONDIMENTS							
	Mushy peas							
	Tomato Ketchup							
	Mayonnaise							
	Tartae Sauce							

Recipe Detail and Cost Card

Glasgow Chip Shop - Recipe detail and Cost Card					
			Selling Price	£	
			Cost	£	
Item:		Menu:	Fixed Cost	%	
Yield:		Portion Size:		Date:	
Ingredients	Quantity	Unit	Cost/Unit		Extention
TOTAL					
METHOD:					

Recipe Detail and Cost Card

Application of Accounting Practices

Perhaps the question is why use costs and financial measures in such an environment. It has been observed that the measurement and monitoring techniques are useful and more reliable when it comes to enabling the setting of kitchen and restaurant budgets. It is also said that for the discerning restaurateur, these tools are vital when it comes to monitoring, controlling and identifying possible issues and adverse trends affecting the business.

Like most aspects of life, many a person has proudly advised that those who, as restaurateurs, fail to plan and monitor, plan to spectacularly fail in the restaurant game. It is no guarantee that those who have taken heed to the aforementioned words of eternal wisdom succeed. They, Restaurateurs that plan, do however, enjoy the support of many a bank manager or investor and can rely on their support should they come across operational obstacles that those who have failed to heed these pearls of wisdom are not privileged.

Applying monitoring and measurement techniques as proposed may highlight the effect of operational practices such as bulk buying and seasonal price changes to ingredients for dishes. Unchecked, some changes may be stealth death cuts that may be highlighted during the restaurant post mortem. It is not uncommon for such price issues to skew the restaurant cash flow and result in death by 'cashless-ness'.

Applied numbers, boring and unemotional as they may be, can also be useful in inadvertently highlighting the effect of quality of ingredients on costs and restaurant performance. An effective system can provide insight as to whether use of higher quality staff and ingredients leads to less waste and more profit of less yield and greater expenses. Using superior quality ingredients may require the use of more skillful and directly more expensive staff as mistakes are relatively costlier. Perhaps the Chef and restaurant philosophy is to engage cheaper labour in the form of junior and less experienced operatives in order to offset the cost of superior ingredients. It is not uncommon in specialist avant-garde establishments that priorities world class ingredients and discriminate on clientele through stroke inducing price policies to employ comparatively low paid staff and all too often unpaid trainees to that effect.

Theft and breakage or shrinkage are human aspects that if not monitored by numbers may go unnoticed. Unfortunately it is human nature, especially under the heat and stress of a professional kitchen and restaurant environment. Staff eating and drinking of prized ingredients can have a major cumulative effect to the restaurants success or failure. This is a classic example, if not numerically monitored, of when stolen goods DO NOT walk out the back or front door of the restaurant. It is extremely difficult to apprehend culprits who rob the restaurant during normal operating hours without arousing suspicion.

Physical locks or chains on cabinets and fridges for high value or hard to acquire ingredients are practical measures that can be very effective. However, third party application of numbers and effective reconciliation through applied monitoring techniques can significantly enhance the probability of success and profitability.

Applied accounting practices such as the ones proposed in this book may also be used to highlight the effect of customer complaints and customer service policies when genuine reasons or otherwise are used to reduce the bill or require no amount to be received in the form of a free meal. This loss of revenue definitely contributes to reduced profitability and relatively increased costs. Both of which are not ideal. In some instances such practices may be attributed to marketing costs for example, however, if left to their own devices, they may operationally be sound policies when in fact they do not fit in with physical budgets and may actually 'break the bank'.

A cancelled reservation may seem innocent enough. In terms of numbers and monitoring, cancellations may represent numerically lost income and possible revenue. When the customer does not show up they do not use up any ingredients that suppliers have to be paid for. These in turn can be offered to other paying customers. However, are customers technically paying for plates of food or space and time in the restaurant dining room or the chef's table? This presents the Restaurateur with the uncomfortable alternative that perhaps the restaurant model is such that their work in producing food or coffee is free and the customer pays for time and experience spent. Perhaps the traditional Chinese buffet can serve as a point of reference.

Apparently, restaurants are dangerous business with ninety percent going bust and one in three failing in the first year. This however, does not hold true for franchises where it is more likely to be one in ten that fall off the mythical cliff into the sea of restaurant oblivion and emotional wrecks.

The difference between the independent operator and the franchisee, according to those in the know, is the level of detail, at times, of the investment into someone else's time spent creating a tried and tested organisational modus operandi as well as painstaking site selection. The concept of franchising is usually developed from the lessons learned from previous entrepreneurs and fashioned into a unique system of measuring and monitoring above average controls and practices both internal and external.

It appears there is no harm in the independent Chef or restaurant adopting attitudes and philosophies that work and keep others in business. A common cause of failure is, among others, undercapitalisation of the venture and a lack of awareness of the need to fastidiously monitor and retain adequate records and working capital. Through costs and financial measures presented in this book, it is possible to avoid certain death by ignorance.

Attention to detail seems to be a trait that everyone seems to have and yet many failed Chefs or restaurateurs believe this does not apply to financial resources and measures. Office paperwork is not the exception to the rule when it comes to restaurants. The restaurateur needs proper and detailed controls over cash management, measurement and handling, portion control, the ever-present cost control practices in food and beverage lines, theft management, as mentioned above, a close eye on investors as well as 'feeding the waste bin' and the inevitable breakages.

The ability to identify and use good cost and financial measures is a sign of great operational management and probably well trained staff. This standard probably sets the tone and philosophy for the restaurant, employee attitudes as well as performance and the resulting happy repeat customers.

Regularly using financial measures may also indicate a level of consistency as a 'mantra' or building block that translates to the food. The resulting reliability and consistency in the eyes of customers is invaluable and possibly pivotal in their decision making process for repeat business. Inconsistency or unreliability has a catastrophic impact on dining experiences and subsequently, the chances of winning awards or more likely survival, even against a franchise.

A Value Proposition (VP) is easier to offer diners when one has proper grasp of what is what especially if this is the end result of sound measures and understanding of ones' costs.

Restaurant operations can be easy money for landlords and local authorities. Unrealistic high rents and occupancy costs seem to be like stealth in the restaurant death game. If not properly measured and monitored along with other costs and financials, will spell a swift and very painful death to many a dream of a budding Chef and restaurateur.

Those who do not recognise the value of costs and financial measures have poor business acumen and probably deserve to fail. The reality is, as much as Chef's dream of creating great culinary master pieces and orgasmic customer experiences, display unworldly passion and commitment, Chefs' need to have a grasp on the realities of business and commerce.

An eye on sound measurement techniques ensures the setting of realistic goals and expectations. This subsequently charts a course for survival and success. Knowing what the Chef has, and at times does not have, ensures they have a hold on their financial clout or lack thereof resulting in better decision making and accurate goal setting plus realistic assumptions on what financial resources One has access to, or not, as the case might be.

The right people, who the Chef needs to find themselves surrounded by, all value and understand the importance and application of costs and financial measures. If One would like the status quo to remain, then One must also speak the language of financial and accounting monitoring in order to give themselves and the restaurant a fighting chance.

A restaurant concept is tricky business. Choosing the wrong option of concept may be administering the fabled kiss of death. However, a look at good costs and financial measures may help change The Restaurateurs mind towards the tunnel with light at the end of all the years of passion and education. Notwithstanding a good and proper test of other factors with market research and respectable analysis.

Some of the answers resulting from application of, once again, costs and financial measures may limit or change other answers to all the realistic assumptions of how much money and resources are needed today and the near as well as distant future, ceteris paribus.

Location, location, location is what some say defines the probability of success for a restaurant. This book loosely asserts a single proposition based on some traditional financial and accounting principles that ought to transcend all the varieties of culinary genius not normally visible to the customers but vital to survival and success. Is now the time to change the old adage of location, to a broader and yet more pragmatic approach which puts forward the notion of Concept, Concept, Concept? Whatever school of thought a Chef pledges their allegiance to, the question still remains, will they succeed? Will they survive? The answer may lie in the final analysis of costs and financial measures. In the absence of an Oracle or Jedi master, tangible results reside in the spirits of measurement and monitoring.

Internal Audit

'Attack is the best form of defense'. This is not a quote from a professional football manager or a Grandmaster of Chess. This is an axiom for the survival of the independent restaurant. Having spent time, which can amount to months planning and executing a cherished idea to become a Chef proprietor or Restaurateur, it would be a great shame to allow the entity to destroy itself from within.

Many examples and incidents of human frailties are sited elsewhere in this book. Perhaps not in great detail, however, it is safe to say that everyone has heard of real life examples of business tragedies caused by moments of human weakness. The Chef or owner must defend the entity that is the independent restaurant against the shortcomings of man. Good financial practices and monitoring will act as a good self-defense mechanism for the business.

This is where the self-imposed internal audit becomes useful. Using forms such as the Butcher test card and Storeroom inventory sheets allow the restaurant to guard against most of the following end results:

- Money unofficially leaving the restaurant till and pilling into employee pockets.

- Once ubiquitous invoice kickbacks

- Over ordering of restaurant ingredients resulting in debilitating and unrecoverable waste

- Organised credit card scams

- Damaging payments to fictitious and bogus suppliers and companies

- The use of counterfeit bank notes and coins

- Ghost payments to employees that have either left the restaurant or even never set foot inside

- Undercharging for friends and family at the till. Even potential 'friends'

- Traumatic fake robberies or phantom theft

- The now infamous expenses fraud practices

- Fraudulent drawings based on feelings of entitlement. This is when an individual fails to acknowledge and adhere to basic fundamental accounting concepts where the Independent restaurant is a business entity distinct from its owners and management. The culprit, a bit harsh but restaurant survival is at stake here, sees themselves as one with the business.

The self-imposed continuous internal auditing seeks to impose internal measures to be taken to safeguard cash and inventory. The cornerstone of which is based on analysing the internal measurement tools and controls as well as systems of properly monitoring financial information and presenting such said reports. This all starts with some physical counting and ensuring that the system works.

GLASGOW CHIP SHOP
Butcher Test Card

Item	Haliburt	Grade	Highland Superior	Date	07-May-14
Quantity	1	Weight	9lbs. 0oz	Average Weight	
Total Cost	£58.50	Unit Cost	£20 per Lb	Supplier	Tartan Fish

Breakdown	No.	Weight - lb.oz	Ratio to Total Weight	Value per Pound	Total Value	Cost of usable Parts Lb	Cost of usable Parts Oz	Portion Size	Portion Cost	Cost Factor Per:- Lb	Cost Factor Per:- Portion
Fat/Bones			50	0.12							
Loss in Trimmings			2.8	0.00							
Useable Parts			47.2					8oz			
TOTAL		9.00	100%								

Notes
At the new price of £15.00 per lb

Cost per lb   Cost per Portion

Storeroom Inventory worksheets

MONTH	APRIL			MAY			JUNE		
ITEMS	Quantity	Price	Amount	Quantity	Price	Amount	Quantity	Price	Amount
Brought Forward			2.00						
Tomato Puree		5.00							
Vinegar(white wine)		1.50							
Vinegar(red wine)		10.00							
Black peppercorns		3.00							
Tinned Chopped tomato		50.00							
TOTAL									

ITEM	PAR STOCK	REORDER POINT	SUBTOTAL	NORMAL USAGE UNTIL DELIVERY	REORDER QUANTITY
PEAS					
TOMATO KETCHUP					
BOTTLED WATER 500ML					
SALT					

Storeroom Inventory worksheets

Relevance of Accounting for the Chef

For the professional chef, recipes are a form of communication and record keeping about ideas and methods that they can use to successfully produce food for customers. In the same way, accounting also provides recipes that are a form or process of communicating financial information about the restaurant as an entity to the Chef, manager, even bank managers and other users including staff.

This specific type of communication is usually in the form of financial statements or graphs that illustrate in universal money terms the economic resources that the Chef and management have under their control. For the Restaurateur or professional Chef, the skill, much the same with cookery recipes, lies in selecting the information that is most useful to the independent restaurant.

The professional Chefs' ability to record, classify and summarise cookery recipes in a scientific manner in terms of weights, measures and degrees of temperature plus time is precisely the same as acts of accounting except that the subject matter, not the ingredients, are in the form of money and are financial in nature plus subsequently interpreting the results of such actions.

Recipes are the language of Chefs the world over in so much as accounting is the language of business. Management accounting allows the chef to communicate with other people inside the restaurant such as co-owners and Sous Chefs for example, and is the basis for restaurant management or most operating decisions. The restaurants financial accounting on the other hand, communicates with people outside the business such as bank managers, suppliers and government agencies.

The Chef's chosen method of internal or management accounting is largely a matter of preference or personal choice. Financial accounting on the other hand, is very structured and subject to many rules. These rules tend to be governed by a body that has jurisdiction and has a say on how reports happen. For the United Kingdom, there is UK GAAP, which is Generally Accepted Accounting Principles. The analogy continues in the form of modern recipes where listing recipes is unofficially standardised, to some extent. The result is that most professional chefs, or anyone for that matter, can look at recorded recipes and understand what's going on in the absence of the originator. This allows for comparison between similar recipes and in financial analysis, similar sized restaurants. To understand how others are performing it is helpful to use similar techniques and comprehend the language of what's going on. Seldom do you find a peerless restaurant that exists in a bubble.

In order to record an effective recipe, there are some features that must be included. When accounting for the restaurant there are inputs that include traditional journal entries, the bookkeeping process and an important feature called the general ledger.

The journal entry can either be a debit or credit and this may consist of many items, including cleaning supplies which however, must not be greater or less than the corresponding total or it may be classed as 'unbalanced'. An example is when debits are greater than credits. The restaurant exists in order to provide a service for paying customers. This sale of plates of food and wine by the chef or proprietor is covered under the Sale of Goods Act

1979 and the resulting payment by customers signifies the completion of the transaction.

The activities of the restaurant and its suppliers are also covered by the above named act, only this time, the Chef is the customer. The recording of these actions in the journal or account ledgers, seeks to show the changes in value that come about from such business activities. The account from which the transaction starts is credited and the account where the transaction ends is debited. If the devil is in the detail then individual transactions may from time to time require more than one debit and credit entry to properly record the changes in value. Professional cookery is littered with many examples of closed circuit heat or flavour exchanges that are a pleasure to be part of, much the same as financial accounting.

The restaurants Balance Sheet is a statement illustrating the net worth at a particular point in time, usually a given date. The Restaurateur uses the balance sheet to record injections and extractions of the restaurants net worth. This is the difference between the value of all the restaurants long term assets and all its external liabilities, what the chef owns and what the chef owes. The period between balance sheets, with the latest being the revised balance sheet, is recorded through journal entries.

Bookkeeping is the recording of the restaurants financial transactions. The Restaurateur should employ the double entry system whereby, for each transaction such as sales, purchase of ingredients, wages paid, the total debits must equal the total credits.

It is important for the Restaurateur to be able to distinguish between the bookkeeping process and the accounting process in which the former is part of the later. In a general sense, recording any financial transaction is a bookkeeping process that the chef is engaged in. This is as straight forward as recording the day-to-day financial transactions of the restaurant.

Most business, especially independent restaurants use what are commonly known as 'day books' which are made up of purchases from suppliers to the restaurant, sales to happy customers as well as receipts and payments. The Restaurateur will do rather well by understanding and ensuring that all transactions are entered into the correct day book. These individual 'books' are then brought to what is known as the Trial Balance stage where the Income Statement and Balance Sheet may be prepared.

The final depository of the restaurants accounting records is the general ledger. As the name suggests, this is the central repository for the restaurant accounting data, and if using software, is transferred from all the restaurants sub-ledgers or sections like accounts receivable, accounts payable, cash management, purchasing of ingredients and sundry, fixed assets and projects such as research and development. This General Ledger is the backbone of the restaurants accounting system which holds financial and non- financial data for the proud independent Chef's restaurant.

Once again, the professional chef takes ingredients, inputs, and successfully turns them into delicious plates or bowls of food, otherwise known as outputs. For the restaurant, accounting outputs are the restaurants financial statements that detail the financial activities of the business, that is, The Chef's independent business. The aforementioned financial statement or report is a formal record of the financial activities of the entire restaurant. This is the presentation of financial information that is relevant to the restaurant in a clear structured manner. Such a statement typically includes four clear sub statements accompanied, usually by a management or chef's discussion and analysis of such said reports. These include the Balance Sheet, as discussed, the Income Statement or Profit and Loss Statement, Cash Flow Statement and finally a statement of Owners Equity if necessary.

The Time Value of Money

Many banks and investors, both of whom are sometimes affectionately known to the Chef or Restaurateurs as 'beloved partners', understand a language called finance. This language, to establish some sort of reference, is usually, well, like most languages, understood by those who have invested their time and passion into learning its composite parts. It is similar to the type of communication usually only found behind the stoves of professional kitchens.

A former chef, Antony Bourdain, in my opinion, describes language in a professional kitchen as some sort of amalgamation of different internationally recognised formal languages, their derivatives and various grunts and groans accompanied by certain 'looks' based on historical shared experiences.

Finance for the Chef, is the reason why they may be able to have a restaurant or enterprise and follow their passion. The classical romanticists may talk of passion arising from helping their grandmothers work magic from their home grown vegetables and local produce while the realists will point, with both index fingers, eyes and an inconspicuous nod to Finance as the underlying reason why they are able to create and artistically produce consistently perfect dishes such as fish and chips with mushy peas.

Usually, chefs spend a lot of time behind the stoves. Unusually, very few work the stove for free. At the end of the day, week or month, there has to be an exchange of money for the time spent. To be honest, unless it is voluntary or a stage, the law requires employees to be paid. However, great chefs appreciate the time value of money.

Understanding the Time Value of Money is not the same as understanding profit or loss, or the cash flow situation. Restaurants are special in that they tend to be cash rich as diners usually pay immediately while suppliers as well as staff are paid thirty to sixty even ninety days later.

It is not essential for the chef to understand Finance Theory and the Time Value of Money, TVM. The ancient bistro, ancestor of the modern restaurant, may have been a part time affair, even a charitable affair whereby travellers where given shelter and fed resulting in a payment in gratitude. Feeding people other than one's family used to be solely a charitable affair. Today it is big business and the modern Chef or Restaurateur and manger needs to keep an eye on the future and look beyond the historic nature of Balance sheets, Income and Cash Flow Statements, especially with the ever changing tax laws, capital equipment and customer expectations.

Every restaurant exists in the world of finance. With an alarmingly high failure rate, the future is not certain for most restaurants beyond the first twelve months. Assuming that the restaurant will exist in its current state in the future, owners or operators can only benefit from understanding the Time Value of Money. This is an amount of money today that has a different buying power, otherwise known as value, for ingredients, supplies and wages for example, than the same amount of money in the future. If a customer is charged £1000.00 for diner today and the restaurant receives it and places it into a bank account earning 5% interest for a period of say twelve months, the Chef will receive £1,050.00 at the end of the term.

Based on the above, the customers £1000.00 today and the Chef's £1050.00 in a year from today have the same value assuming 5% interest. The good customer's £1000.00 invested for a period of one year at 5% interest has a fantastic future value of £1050.00 for the clever Chef.

Restaurants benefit because they receive money today from diners tonight when its future value is subject to inflation and generating additional income by earning interest, possibly before it is spent or used. The 'value' of money to the chef will change because there is an opportunity to earn interest on the money and also because inflation will drive the prices of items such as ingredients, for example potatoes up.

By properly applying the various financial measurement and monitoring techniques, the chef or owner is able to accurately know how much money is available and the impact of interest on said sum assuming inflation is neutral or held constant. Any chef who cares about their work and livelihood is likely to be interested in the future, not just for the change of seasons and arrival of new ingredients, but also for the value of the likely stream of diners' payments in the future.

This may especially be important as the restaurant may make payments long into the future after the goods or ingredients have already been spent. Naturally, this only applies if there is good credit and monthly salaried employees. It is also necessary to plan for taxation and appraise any options for capital expenditure, or not.

Knowledge of finance to a greater extent is all too often overlooked by chefs or owners as the funds to start or maintain the restaurant usually come from friends and family or a bank personal loan. As there are usually less strings attached to this sort of fund raising, less evidence of financial and accounting competence is required. Basic information will usually suffice and not much emphasis placed on financial details due to the chef or owner's talent, passion, dedication and long held dreams.

The cost of capital is lightly addressed at the face value and the capital assets of the restaurant are acquired on a 'is there enough cash in the bank account to buy a new gizmo' criteria at the chef's sole discretion.

Independent Restaurant Cash Flow Statement

A restaurant is often described as a cash-rich business. This means that, provided the restaurant has customers, there will be money going through the tills. The cash flow statement illustrates the independent restaurants liquidity and ability to keep operating, otherwise called solvency.

Like most independent restaurants, the money received from customers and coming into the restaurant is known to the chef as Cash Inflow and the other side of the coin or fillet of sole, so to speak, money heading out of the Restaurateurs business is called Cash Outflow. To accurately reflect the impact of all the comings and goings of cash in the restaurant, the fourth and final statement, known as the Cash flow statement is used.

The above named statement is a very important tool for the restaurant as it reports the cash basis on the previously mentioned trio of financial activities. To recap once again, these activities are divided into Operating, Investing and finally Financing Activities. The independent restaurants may engage in other non-cash activities but these are usually reported in the footnotes of the Financial Report.

To operate efficiently and effectively, the Chef needs to be aware of whether it is possible or not and if so, how easy it is to change cash flows to keep the restaurant operating in the near and distant future. The independent restaurant may hold cash in assets such as stock in the form of ingredients or more profitable financial instruments with a broker or bank. The statement of cash flows provides information that assists in the decision making process to ensure cash, or the lifeblood of any business, is available to pay bills such as taxes and wages when due.

The Cash Flow statement for the restaurant also manages to reconcile the cash balance and provide a connection between one balance sheet and the next. As a result, this statement is a motion statement.

As the independent restaurant world moves at quite a brisk pace, the chef's statement of cash flows allows the relevant people to be able to evaluate changes in assets, the business liabilities and equity. This is a useful financial statement for many a Restaurateur that wants to evaluate their own performance against those of their peers as it does not include allocations such as depreciation or write-offs.

Much the same as the Income Statement, a statement of Cash flows also reflects a named accounting period and is usually a summary of cash transactions. The trio of above named financial activities are shown as line movements for the restaurant as either cash in-flows or cash out-flows. It is important to note that the term cash, for all intents and purposes is used to include items that are generally accepted as cash and what the restaurant may have as near cash, or cash equivalents.

Currency, pound sterling in coins and bank notes held by the restaurant in the tills and the office safe is considered cash. This also includes any amount in the restaurant bank accounts. The professional Chef or restaurateur will do well to appreciate cash as a medium of exchange. As it says on the bank notes, "I promise to pay the bearer on demand". The restaurant is assumed to have a fiduciary relationship with customers in whom the establishment places complete confidence in the Diner with regard to the diner and subsequent payment for said consumption of food and beverages and payment in cash, or equivalent.

The independent restaurant generates cash primarily from the sale of food and beverages or the hire of space and staff for external functions. It also generates cash in-flows from the occasional sale of assets and the likely borrowings from commercial banks, suppliers as well as investment and contribution from owners and stakeholders.

As mentioned elsewhere, the restaurant uses cash to pay suppliers and pay for its other operating and capital expenditure. The cash out-flow also includes payments for liabilities and possible dividends to owners, should they so wish. In a nut shell, the statement of cash flows illustrates information on the independent restaurants sources and uses of associated cash and cash equivalents. The latter is widely defined as marketable securities with a maturity of less than three months. The Chef or Restaurateur will do well to enquire about these financial instruments and possibly investigate The International Accounting Standards (IAS) 7 Statement of Cash Flows.

It may be safe to say that every independent restaurant operates a small system that allows the management to keep a small amount of cash onsite for day to day expenses known as the petty cash. This system may resemble the Imprest system in which the management has a 'float' or set amount, for example, one hundred pounds. This set amount is usually balanced or replenished by taking funds from another of the restaurants cash accounts, usually the main bank account. This is a form, be it small in comparison, of a financial accounting system.

Using the Imprest system to manage petty cash ensures discipline among the restaurants responsible party as only an equivalent amount of the money that has been spent during that period can be replaced or replenished. This system also insures that only the starting amount of what the chef or restaurateur has in the place in the petty cash account, or physical box can be used and not more.

    The above system allows the Chef or restaurateur to summarise the fluctuations of the petty cash amount and ensure that the numbers do not make the users of the financial information feel confused and dizzy. The statement of cash flows for the independent restaurant should enable a connection and understanding of the business operations.

Glasgow Chip Shop

Independent Restaurant Cash Flow Statement

Year Ended April 4 2013

	£	£
Cash Flows from Operating Actives:		
Operating Income (EBIT)	305,050	
Depreciation Expense	3,000	
Loss on Sale of refrigeration equipment	250	
Increase in Accounts receivable	-4,000	
Decrease in Prepaid expenses	310	
Decrease in Account Payable	-4,801	
Decrease in Accrued Expenses	-273	
NET CASH FLOW FROM OPERATING ACTIVITIES		299,53(
Cash Flows from Investing Activities:		
Sale of refrigeration equipment	12,800	
Purchase of equipment	-15,000	
NET CASH FLOW FROM INVESTING ACTIVITIES		-2,20(
Cash flows from Financing Activities:		
Payment of dividends	-102,870	
NET CASH FLOW FROM FINANCING ACTIVITES		-102,87(
NET CHANGE IN CASH		194,46(
BEGINNING CASH BALANCE		83,12(
ENDING CASH BALANCE		277,59:

The Independent Restaurant Balance Sheet

The balance sheet of the independent restaurant which uses or aims to use proper accounting methods has been introduced as one of the restaurants four basic financial statements. In actual fact, the balance sheet is the summary of the financial balances of the restaurant in all its forms of ownership. From the Sole trader to business partnerships, with limited liability or not, as well as other forms of organisational structure and ownership.

The restaurant balance sheet is also known by another more descriptive name which is a Statement of Financial Position. This is what it is because it illustrates the restaurants financial position and whether it is trading solvent or not.

As a tool for the restaurateur, the balance sheet is unique in that it is more like an x-ray that reveals the financial position of the restaurant at a particular point in time. It is a metaphorical photograph that reflects the financial position at the end of the restaurants business on the day the balance sheet is run or compiled.

The illustrated example of the Independent Glasgow Chip shop shows the restaurants assets, liabilities current and non-current, and stockholders' equity at a precise point in time. The assets are the total resources of the restaurant including cash, accounts receivable and notes, at the same time. The liabilities include anything the restaurant owes to someone else including debt, interest payments and mortgages.

From the Balance Sheet, current assets for the independent restaurant are usually described as assets with a formal value available to the Chef or restaurateur in the short term within a year, for example cash. The other part of the assets element is the fixed assets. As the assets are assessed relative to time, the latter are assumed to have a long term value of more than a year and the list includes such items as restaurant leases, stoves and fridges plus computing and printing equipment.

The owners' equity or stockholders equity explains or shows the ownership interest in the restaurant. Clearly put, this is usually what is left over after subtracting liabilities from assets.

The balance sheet of the Glasgow Chip shop shows the size and extent of the independent restaurants or, depending on the type of legal entity, the owners' financial obligations. This information is useful to the Chef or Restaurateur as it illustrates whether the business can be grown or not. If the debts are too high, as an example, it is usually not advisable to attempt to grow the restaurants business.

There is also what is known as Liquidity. This is a measure of how easy and quickly it is to convert restaurants assets into cash. This is because cash is the more readily accepted method of payment for any of the restaurants liabilities. If the Chef or Restaurateur has no access to cash when bills are due the restaurant has technically bled out and may not survive.

The most liquid assets such as cash on hand or in the bank are usually listed first followed by near cash items such as inventory. The idea is that the Chef or Restaurateur or even the investors may feel more comfortable with the restaurants resources invested in good assets that are easily convertible into cash and not hold too much inventory in case of an unexpected expense or incident such as fridge malfunction or burst water mains.

Of great interest to the Chef may be the final part of the balance sheet which tells the story of the book value of the owners' stake in the restaurant business. This may be of interest if someone else intends to appraise the value of any investment they may make in terms of a price for any share of the restaurant.

Glasgow Chip Shop
Independent Restaurant Balance Sheet
As At 18 April 2010

		£	£
Current Assets			
	Cash at Bank	200	
	Inventory	437.1	
	Debtors	62.9	
	TOTAL CURRENT ASSETS		700
Non-Current Assets			
	Buildings	20,000.00	
	Plant and equipment	4,210.25	
	Vehicles (Motorcycle)	90.75	
	TOTAL NON-CURRENT ASSETS		24,300.00
TOTAL ASSETS			25,000.00
Current Liabilities			
	Credit cards	37	
	Creditors	2,000.00	
	Tax payable	963.5	
	TOTAL CURRENT LIABILUTIES		3,000.50
Non-current liabilities			
	Long term loans		15,000.00
TOTAL LIABILIES			18,000.50
Owners' Equity			
	Capital	3,000.00	
	Retained Earnings	2,000.00	
	Current earnings	1,000.00	
TOTAL OWNERS EQUITY			6,000.50

Independent Restaurant Income Statement

For the Chef and Restaurateur, the income statement illustrates the independent restaurants revenues, for example from customers and its expenses for a specific period. This statement is another part of the team of base level statements for the restaurants set of financial communication. This statement reflects the operating performance of the independent restaurant.

Also known as the Statement of Financial Performance as well as the Earnings Statement. In addition to the above reflection, it also shows any vicissitudes and impact of such changes in the restaurants assets and obligations. The income statement has another name, Statement of Operations or Revenue Statement.

The operating statement, unlike its contrasting snap shop brother the balance sheet, represents a period of time. The statement of the independent restaurants earnings is prepared on what is known as an accrual basis.

The restaurants profit and loss statement, also known as the income statement, illustrates for the chef the revenues recognised for a said specific period and the associated costs and restaurant expenditure used to obtain the revenues, including waste or write-offs. This even includes intangible items such as depreciations and amortisation of the restaurants assets as well as government taxation.

Vital to the Chef or Restaurateur is knowledge of whether the restaurant made or lost money during the said period being illustrated by the profit and loss statement. This income statement shows how the restaurants daily revenue from Diners and sale of beverages plus service before legitimate expenses are removed, produces the business net income. The aforementioned net Income or net Profit is what is shown after all the restaurants revenues and subsequent expenses have been taken into consideration. This exercise for the restaurant shows the relevance of operating and non-operating activities and illustrates the performance of the restaurants primary business activities.

Glasgow Chip Shop

Income Statement
Year Ended 20**

Sales
- Food — £
- Beverage — £
- Total Sales — £

Cost of Sales
- Food — £
- Beverage — £
- Total Cost of Sales — £

GROSS PROFIT — £

Controllable Expenses
- Salaries and Wages — £
- Employee Benefits — £
- Other Controllable Expenses — £

TOTAL CONTROLLABLE EXPENSES — £

INCOME BEFORE OCCUPANCY COSTS — £

- Occupancy costs — £
- Interest — £
- Depreciation — £
- TOTAL — £

RESTAURANT PROFIT — £

Computer and Mobile Application Programmes

The idea is that the Restaurateur should think of modern restaurant software and mobile device applications as an addition to the traditional financial monitoring and measurement. An attempt to extrapolate as much relevant information as possible out of the systems. In so much as the systems are faster, more accurate and potentially economical, there still needs to be the bread and butter inputs based on the restaurants ability to keep its doors open and the oven turned on.

The potential of software and Apps is vast. Only an 'old school' and 'traditional' professional chef or restaurateur would ignore this universally accepted and applied fact. Having said that, the sheer size and spectrum of what is available is a daunting prospect. This is in addition to the fact that the functions and social impact are in a state of constant change and improvement.

Is it only a matter of time before such programmes are able to peel and blanche the exact amount of potatoes needed for tomorrows diner service? In the meantime, human emotion prevails and customer whims aplenty and continue to provide many a professional chef with a conundrum. However, most industries can survive without computer software and apps in any shape or form. They will however struggle to remain competitive if the objective is to become profitable and remain a professional operation.

The major benefit of software and apps is that they allow everyone associated with the restaurant such as employees, suppliers and customers to communicate more effectively and efficiently as well as stay in business during such competitive times. One crucial mistake made in many kitchens is assuming that Software and Applications are just modern filling and storage cabinets to be one day handed over to the accountant and Revenue and Customs investigators.

The speed at which any form of communication now transpires has been accepted as the norm and significantly reduced the amount of time that anyone may choose to wait before providing feedback and engaging with others. Restaurant Software and Apps facilitate keeping up with any requests for financial dialogue and quicker diagnosis of organisational health. Like most conditions, survival may depend upon early diagnosis and treatment. Fast and effective measurement using good financial management practices may make all the difference.

Once again, Software and Apps help the independent Chefs place all their eggs in the proverbial basket and keep the good eye on them. It is easier to view organised data and possibly identify correlations and often mutually exclusive events plus trends before they become catastrophic. Such items allow chefs to have more time to perform stock-in-trade tasks.

The key to restaurant Software and Apps, like most tools in business is to get organised, research what is available based on the Chefs' independent type of restaurant, knowledge of the current market and trends as well as understanding and clarity about what the professional Chef would like the programmes to do. Knowing the basis of what is going on often avoids confusion and failure.

Beware the cost. Setting up an Excel or Word worksheet and investing a few hours to set up functions may be cost effective and more than adequate, even for the humble Glasgow Chip Shop.

Software for software's' sake is usually not a good idea. Before such items existed, many a Restaurateur still operated their own establishment. Perhaps not at optimum efficiency or competitiveness, seeing as these attributes where not necessarily a pre-requisite for survival in times gone by. It is still possible to use paper and napkins as modus operandi. However, it may be hard to find a recommendation for this method of operating in isolation when it comes to financial management.

In Conclusion, perhaps more importantly, please seek independent professional advice before investing in any financial tools, products and services. This content is supplied on an information only basis. Naturally, Restaurateur will assume ownership and responsibility for any possible outcome of their actions, or lack thereof.

'Je vous adresse mes meilleurs voeux'

www.ingramcontent.com/pod-product-compliance
Lightning Source LLC
Chambersburg PA
CBHW072233170526
45158CB00002BA/875